pr

A MOUNTAIN'S IDEA OF TIME

"True poetry is what happens when one is consistently, even religiously, engaged in paying attention to the world with every passing moment. Charles Finn is one of the great examples of what this commitment looks like on the page, his attentiveness to the spirit in experience evident with every poem.

What a joyful immersion! Savoring these poems, I found myself reflecting on old songs that are so sad my heart is somehow uplifted, as encountered on long drives across prairie anything but empty. Finally, I smiled at Finn's nod to a kind of original instruction we might receive from a cherished elder. 'Take note of everything,' he writes. 'Be kind to animals.' These poems are devotions to the moment to moment gift of being alive."

—**Chris La Tray,** Métis storyteller and Montana poet laureate.

" 'I'd like to live at the pace of stones,' Charles Finn writes in this magnificent new book of poems. He gives us a gift of time in which to dwell, to breathe, to 'pull the dark blossom of death' over us, to 'put ourselves in the path of beauty, and curl up for a nap in a coyote's den.' *A Mountain's Idea of Time* is truly wonderful. These poems are deep yet lightly-footed."

—**Gretel Ehrlich,** author of *The Solace of Open Spaces* and *Unsolaced.*

"Everything I need—now—is here in these poems. The pure joy of perfect words. 'Baby-faced peaches.' The healing power of astonishment: 'The sky / ridiculous with clouds.' I read and shake my head in wonder—Yes, this is right. This is true. This is the beauty I had forgotten. Charles Finn's poetry is a miracle of gratitude that will save lives in dangerous times to come."

—**Kathleen Dean Moore,** author of *Earth's Wild Music*

"A fragrance of farewell wafts through *A Mountain's Idea of Time* as poet Charles Finn, in his true hand, brings his most treasured Northwestern places and memories to the page—from the 'oil-drop eyes' of the yellow-pine chipmunk to the 'chapel of birdsong, the temple of my renewing;' from the wistfulness of used bookstores in 'Vellichor,' the heartrending elegy, 'Song Sparrow,' or the exquisite expression of love in 'The Vase,' 'She laughs as if arranging her voice like flowers.' "

—**Ellen Waterston,** Oregon Poet Laureate,
author of *We Could Die Doing This* and *Hotel Domilocos, Poems*

"These poems by Charles Finn are part of the art that is necessary for survival in these days of digital overload. Finn takes us on a journey to all his favorite places in the Northwest and in these poems, we get to sit with him at the edge of a river or when he is holding a newly dead song sparrow in the palm of his hand. When he says 'Hold your breath, just now a red Fox/Is slipping through the snowberry,' we do. Finn reminds us of what it means to love this fragile world."

—**Mary Jane Nealon,** author of *Rogue Apostle* and *Immaculate Fuel*

"In Charles Finn's deft poetry, we are asked to pay attention—to the spots on fawns and rainbow trout, to the passage of time, to wonderment and wildness. In a culture that moves quickly, Finn reminds us of the joy and longing that can greet us each day, in each moment, in poems that sing and shine across this collection. Whether climbing mountains, wading in streams, or thinking as the world rolls by, Finn reminds us that we all have our gods, and that it's important to follow them in a world where every precious thing is at stake."

—**Taylor Brorby,** author of *Boys and Oil:
Growing Up Gay in a Fractured Land*

A MOUNTAIN'S IDEA *of* TIME

Also by Charles Finn

Wild Delicate Seconds: 29 Wildlife Encounters

On a Benediction of Wind: Poems and Photographs of the American West
(winner 2022 Montana Book Award)

The Art of Revising Poetry (co-editor)

We Are All God's Poems (co-editor)

A MOUNTAIN'S IDEA *of* TIME

poems

Charles Finn

CHATWIN BOOKS
Seattle, 2025

A Mountain's Idea of Time, by Charles Finn

Published by Chatwin Books

ISBN: 978-1-6339-8182-9

This author's work was made possible in part by a grant from the Montana Arts Council, an agency of the State Government.

Edited by Phil Bevis, Molli Corcoran, and Anna Brunner
Cover artwork "Refuge, Bitterroots" by Bobbie McKibbin
Author photo by Barbara Michelman, with special thanks to Barbara for also photographing the cover artwork for this book
Book design and typesetting by Annie Brulé

Set in Espiritu and Change typefaces

Designed, printed and bound in the greater Seattle area

Published by Chatwin Books
www.chatwinbooks.com

for Joyce

CONTENTS

⁂

CONTENTS

⁂

CONTENTS

⁜

"Imagine inventing yellow."

—M.C. Richards

Driving the Backroads of Montana

Driving the backroads of Montana
Gravel unspools to the horizon

Fields of wind and wheat surround me
I've got all the good long day left to drive.

My dog is asleep beside me
There's a creek up ahead that I know

Where cottonwoods and trout lounge in the shadows
As good a place as any to lie down.

But I've stopped to lean on a rail fence
A horse walking toward me out of the fog

It nuzzles my coat pockets for apples
Warm alfalfa breath on my neck

The ache and loneliness of living made bearable
I pat the horse's neck and it knows.

for Martha Scanlan

Those Were the Days

Do you remember a time
When a single dragonfly
Could make your day
And ears of corn truly listened
When autumn leaves and earthworms
Gave the best advice.
Do you remember
How you talked with cows and bees
The maple tree down the street
Or maybe just sat there
A bump on a log
Swinging your feet for hours.
Now the years pass in a blink
The world shrinks and we travel
Further and further away
From ourselves. Just last night
I tried to wish upon a star, and failed.
What we lose growing up is everything.

Simple Pleasures

I would like to live at the pace of stones
Have a mountain's idea of time
Spend my days in the company of shadows
Companion to inchworm, turtle, and tree.

It's hard, wouldn't you agree?
Everything happening so fast
And knowing so little
Only that life must end
Yet here we are
You, me, every last one of us
Forever and always
Just getting started.

Which is why I come down to the river
Simple pleasures, that's what it tells me
A kingfisher spiking into the water
A cottonwood leaning in
Trout asleep in the shadows.
I close my eyes, let my mind
Drift downstream.
Breathe.

Where It All Begins

Hunger is where it all begins
The owl's silent flight, the heron's
Unswerving patience, the mountain lion's

Soft tread. Hunger is the leap of salmon
Leap of deer, the eagle's binocular stare
It's what grew the bear into the bear.

Hunger designed the brown swimsuit
Of the beaver, it created the mountain goat
And the mountain goat's casual attitude

Around gravity. Hunger is the world
At its best, the perfect leveling field
Hope for another day. Look around

Hunger doesn't leave one of us alone
It taught the salamander to lose its tail
It tells the praying mantis to devour her lover.

We All Have Our Gods

We all have our gods
The first robin of spring
Sunlight through the pines
The fall of a favorite river or stream
Over time-worn stones.

There are perfectly rainbowed trout
Spots on newborn fawns, days
No one in their right mind but a duck
Would go out to play in the rain.

I was out walking today
Worms on the sidewalk
Squirrels grooming their tails
It was easy to see
Something important going on.

Trust me, there's good at every turn
The red-tailed hawk, wind
Over fields of just ripe wheat.
There are baby-faced peaches
And huckleberries in need of picking.

So go ahead, pray to whichever god
Makes you the most happy
Me? I'll take that chevron of geese
Just now, over your left shoulder
Crossing in front of the moon.

And So It Is

And so it is and is and is
And always will be
This river, this lake
Chapel of birdsong
Temple of my renewing.

I come here early mornings
Take my seat on the folding chair of Now
First light blushing in the east
Night's blue-bruised sky
Quietly healing.

Oh, I know, life is nothing more
Than the skip of a stone on the water
The fall of a leaf.
I know love and loss
Are two sides of the very same coin.
Like the river gods of old
I wade into the water
Up to my knees, my waist
Wash my hands, my face.

Wonder begets wonder
I turn and turn and turn
The evidence all around me.
Blackbirds top the cattails
Mice breathe and mountains heave
A muskrat carves a wake, everything
I need ever know, right here, right now
Stirring in the tails of the trout
The rustle of leaves, passing
In the ragged
Torn brilliance of clouds.

Prairie Wind

This morning the wind like a train
The sky a runaway horse
Small birds being tossed like confetti
And the willows bent to their god.

We all know the old joke
If the wind ever stops
All the chickens will fall over.
We've all been schooled in updrafts and down.

I don't want to hear it.

I want to hear Grandmother travels
Five hundred miles to touch my face
That Grandfather pats my back.
I want to breathe what lifts hawks' wings!

Oh, this prairie wind, how it makes my eyes water
Luffs my soul. Tell me it carries the first songs
Stories never told outside a circle of fire, tales
Only a coyote could know.

Friend, are you weary like me?
Step outside. Take the names of all the souls
Into your lungs. Hold them there.
Let them go.

VELLICHOR*

She'd spend hours wandering the aisles, mouthing the titles of forgotten stories, leafing through the bitter sweetness of old cookbooks. She loved the soul-sad stacks, their wistfulness, the forlorn atmosphere of unturned pages. There was the lazy stroll, the tipped head, the joy of hooking an index finger over a threadbare spine. Lick of thumb, turn of page, glasses balanced on the end of her nose, aren't we all just a little dog-eared too? Behind the cash register, first editions under lock and key. Upstairs science fiction and the wood floors creak. In the children's corner Dr. Seuss and the deep suffering of the world forgotten. Autumn days she liked best, rain outside, rain in her heart, pebbles of rain sliding down the window panes like tears on a cheek. With a copy of Rumi and another of Blake, she'd settle into the poetry corner, where, turning to the tranquility of the napping cat, a delicious weariness overtook her blood and bones.

***vel**-ə-kōr (noun): *the strange wistfulness of used bookstores.*

Well Met Sunshine

Well met sunshine
pale ray on forest floor
small spotlight on lichen and leaves.
Dark here the shadows
the green moss gathered round.
How far you have come
how pleasant, how proud.
Precious then this moment
your journey over, and me
a minute here, a minute there
I would have missed you.

Dreaming

I am dreaming I am Stone
hard, round, smooth
a river stone, washed by River
polished by Moonlight.

I am dreaming I am Bird
hollow bones, twig legs
voice like a song.
I stand on Stone's back
in the middle of River, singing.

I am dreaming I am River
Stone in my middle, Bird in my ear
Fish swimming inside me
Deer coming to drink.

I am dreaming I am Deer, Fish, Forest
Mountain, River, Stone, Tree.
I am dreaming, I am dreaming, I am dreaming.
Please, do not wake me.

Listen Closely

I am sending you the sounds
Of the forest at night

I am opening the window
Letting in the questions of owls

The gnawing of mice. I am wrapping you
In the coughs of mountain lions

Snoring of bears, in the whisper of grass parting
Making way for a mink.

Cup your ear, turn your heart
To what commands you.

Can you hear the bark of the ponderosa
Growing in puzzles?

Can you hear the tiny thunder
Of rabbit hearts pounding?

Hold your breath, just now a red fox
Is slipping through the snowberry.

Listen! There it is!
Moonlight caught in its tail.

Say My Name

Summer late afternoon
Slow descent of sun
All the time in the world
Stretching by in the shadows.

From the willows mourning doves call
And the souls of the dead
Cock their ears, the high clouds curdled
Turning pink.

There's the odor of the neighbor's grill
And his newly cut lawn
There's the gravel crunch of cars
Going by on the road behind.

Lavender blooms, roses climb
She takes a sip of wine
Sees the blood rushing behind her eyes
"Say my name."

Later that evening the stars
Blink their Morse code
Behind them the dark
A language we will all one day speak.

There's no telling
Who, what, where, when, why, or how
He turns to her, leans close
And whispers.

Coyote

What pass as miracles
Are few and far between
When in reality
It should be every damn thing.
Yesterday I watched a coyote
Cross an icebound river
He stopped to turn and look at me
I couldn't help it, I waved a small, stupid wave.
Don't get me wrong
The world is a puzzle
Not even the wisest can solve.
I watched Coyote up a hill, down a hill
Jogging along in the pale evening light.
There are so many ways to be a friend
And never as much time as we think.
So many ways to say, "Here I am!"
One day I hope to follow Coyote
Back to his den, curl up with him
On the cold, damp earth
Breathe the air he breathes, dream
The dreams he dreams, just Coyote
The river, and me.

Geese, North in the Spring

Maybe they know and maybe they don't
Maybe love never had an answer

I think they drain themselves of everything
And follow their hearts to the end.

Days of iron skies don't deter them
The weight of moonlight never gets mentioned

It's the doggedness of doing this one thing
That amazes—a longing like no other.

Rivers, coast lines, mountain tops and valleys
Magnetic fields. Do they know?

Or do they fly, as all must fly
On abject faith.

Song Sparrow

When the little ones fall, it seems to hurt the most. —*Anna Page*

Now I am picking it up
Now I am placing it
In the palm of my hand
Now I am crossing
The wind-filled field.

What an invention is death
And what a small coat
Of delicate feathers.

Today I took
The small, still warm body
A tiny song sparrow
Two tablespoons
In the palm of my hand
And buried it out back
In a field of wind
And young weeds.

I said, now I am opening the earth
I said, now I am placing him carefully within
I said, now I am pulling the dark blossom of death
Over his head—it was all I could do—
And the wind walked me home
A tiny warmth
And sadness
Still cupped and floating
In the palm of my hand.

Faith

Birds know
stepping from the nest
for the very first time
the meaning
of opening their wings.

Yellow, a Poem for the Blind

A blind man once asked me
What does yellow look like
And I told him

Yellow is the feeling you get
When you're five-years-old
Sliding down a slide

It's the first time a girl
Says your name, or a boy
Holds your hand

It's like swimming downstream
Like floating in the ocean
Like skipping, like a hug

That's yellow. Birds sing in yellow, I said
Good news is yellow, yellow I told him
Is the thing you would do

All day, every day, if you could
And I watched him walk away
A new bounce in his step

Smile blooming on his face
Which, I kid you not
He turned toward the sun.

The Tiny Nail

A painting hangs on a wall.
It has hung there for years.
A tiny nail holds it.
People pass the painting every day.
They never see the painting
It has become part of the wall.
The frame of the painting is dusty
And behind it a rectangle
Where the paint hasn't faded.
Meanwhile, everywhere outside the painting
The world is turning, and I, like you
Like every person alive
Have been charged with telling the truth.
For nights I have lain awake thinking about this
Inside and outside the painting
There is so much we don't know—so much.
Which is why I have decided
In the morning, I will take the painting down.
I will expose the tiny nail.

THE WEIGHT OF THE ORDINARY

and so it is here in our home
the plates stacked so neatly
the spoons doing their thing
socks matched and paired
jackets hung in darkness
that we live our lives of quiet glory
passing the days in gladness and wonder
the weight of the ordinary a gift and a blessing
a hand on a shoulder, a kiss when in need.

Gifts I Have Been Given

Once, standing on the shore
Of a frozen pond at night
Rising from under the ice
The sound of turtles singing.

Once, far back in the woods
Resting against a pine
The porcupine above me dreaming
I was its brother.

And once sitting by a river
Deep in my heart the river's delight
In the hundred salmon noses I saw
Pushing upstream.

What counts as luck
Is often being awake.
Put yourself in the path of beauty
And you can't go wrong.

For years I thought myself unworthy
Until the day a black-capped chickadee
Landed on my shoulder
Whispered sweet nothing in my ear.

Sunday Morning

A communion wafer
Is the exact size
Of a full moon.
A priest wears baggy sleeves
Like a magician.

It's Sunday morning
I'm ten-years-old
Speed-saying my prayers
And lying in confession
My best friend
Two pews in front of me
Wiggling his ears.

But now the priest
Is mumbling his Latin
And my father is standing up
His chin is clean shaven
And my mother is standing up
She's wearing a pink dress.
There are twelve stations of the cross
And we line up like beggars.

When the body and blood
Of our lord Jesus Christ
Sticks to the roof of my mouth
I peel him off with a finger.
God knows the path I am on.

Grandson

And just like that
the whole grand bazaar of childhood
spread out before me
an entire world of trees
waiting to be climbed.

We were jumping in puddles
drinking from hoses
Riding bikes, "Look! No hands!"
as hand-in-hand we went.

Oh, the clandestine joy
of lying on my back
watching clouds
having hour-long conversations
with frogs and bees.

No, I wasn't growing old
I was growing young again
with my grandson
skipping stones.

for Ezekiel Wellington Charles Brandt

Memory's Anvil

Somewhere far, far out
On the Montana plains
Left in the attic
Of an old stone farmhouse
Hangs a broken-necked fiddle
With mouse-gnawed soundboard
And missing strings.

I hear it most nights.

The scored dirt floor below
Is rutted, the footsteps gone
There's less and less
For the walls to be concerned about
To say nothing of the wind
Come all these miles.

Nor would I call it a dance exactly
What the faded curtains get up to
But we all live lives of ambition
And I'll wager they're doing their best
Like the rain on the roof
A welcome percussion, and the dust
That comes down from the rafters
To do-si-do.

How I like to lie awake and listen
Cry a little if truth be told
Imagining the tunes that fiddle played
When the music of bare feet and thigh slap
Fought off drought and golf ball-sized hail
Filling this old house
Not a little unlike prayer.

Route 20 Barn

Standing profoundly graceful in the center of its field, slouched like some kind of colossal beast, it leans its great and sleeping weight against the sunshine. See the paw of gravity heavy upon it, the architect of Time tearing it down. Stop the car. Get out. Walk three times around it. Put your hands to the quietude of disuse. Look how the sun has chosen from its infinite palette this slim variety of browns, how the wind has pianoed the shingles. Don't be afraid, step through the shadows. Inside, a fretwork of beams like the rib cage of an animal. Now climb up. Scrape the pigeon shit from the rafters. There, there in the geometry of fir beams and oak dowels, a cup of dried mud and four speckled eggs. The swallows! The swallows are back.

Lest We Forget

The creaky wisdom of trees
The jokes stones tell about time
The pride mountains feel
Looking down their valleys
Each and every story told
In the eyes of animals.

The First Time We Met

The first time we met
Hope was a word
I kept in my pocket
Like a chocolate
Something saved
For a better day.
Then in the twilight
Your heart a trout surfacing
To the fly-cast of my love
My heart a tiny bird opening
Its beak to be fed.
It was October
Red and yellow leaves
Disappearing downstream.
Do you believe in miracles?
I believe in miracles.
A violin played
The sidewalks became beautiful
A stranger passing said, "If not now, when?"
As you took my face in your hands
Kissed me for all that you're worth.

Snail Mail

This snail mail
This crinkled and white
Antique we call paper
Carried to me by the most
Human of hands
Arrived today from its
Jet-lagged long journey
Reading nonetheless
Love for its wear.
You see I have never
Saved an electronic transmission
As I do your small hand
These colorful and scribbled
Crayons of love
Your almost too real
Cutout velvet young hearts
Your kinked and backwards
S's and e's
They have brightened my day
Me, and old and bone white refrigerator
Graced by your art.

Coming Off Whiskey (the horse)

It hurt to laugh
Eight broken ribs and a collapsed lung
A horse wreck if you've ever seen one.

Four days in hospital
They took away his spurs
And not a pretty nurse to be found.

Still, he thanks his lucky stars
For oxycodone, asks for his hat
And swears he'll get back on.

for Neil Browne

In the Café

In the café of ordinary cups and saucers
On the corner of Nowhere and Main
In the city of Nothing Much Happens
They come for weak coffee
Tiny cinderblocks of sugar
White top hats of cream
Wedges of starchy apple pie.
They come for the company
Of ketchup bottles they spank
And the yellow mustard they squeeze
Each struggling in
Dressed like a napkin
Tossed down after a meal.
You see them ten at night, three in the morning
Two p.m., alone, avuncular
The meniscus of their loneliness
Trembling to overflow
Here in the world of trying to remember
How speech is formed
By ordering from the waitress
Who is fifty, sashays, and—*bless her, bless her*—
Brings them refills
Calls them all "Dearie"
Sometimes even "Honey"
As she sets the cup down.

Footprints in the Sand

She wore white cotton dresses printed with roses
and sandals that fastened at the ankle.
Summer evenings she'd walk barefoot along the beach
singing to herself, "*Alouette, gentille alouette, Alouette...*,"
swinging the sandals from her fingers
and laughing the laugh of a tiny bird.
This was where the old men and women liked to gather
sipping their wine and smoking
the last of the day's sun
like a warm hand pressed to their faces.
She'd walk along the beach and sing
and liked the deep pockets of their eyes
and the tattered cardigans they wore.
It was a ritual to pass before them
a reminder of beauty and youth.
The old men appreciated this
but the women looked away
pretending they didn't see.
The young woman walked the beach
put her tiny feet in the sand
and somewhere in the city
a white cat curled into a ball.
Then, later, when the lights were out
when everyone was asleep
when the moon said to the tide, "Come. Go,"
that's when you'd see them, the old women
curved spines and walnut faces, arthritic hands
bending to take off their shoes
placing the gnarled root masses of their feet
exactly in the footprints she'd made.

Vase

I step into the room, a party
food, drink, people I know
and there in the kitchen a woman
like a dark vase, beautiful, and set apart.
I think she would be too frightening to hold
even touch, lest I break her
and I commit my hands to my pockets.
But there is no such hope for my eyes
and like with any beautiful thing
they are drawn back to her all evening.
I watch her from across the room
she laughs as if arranging her voice
like flowers.

for Joyce

All Together Now

Leave the darkness to the crickets
They know what they're doing
Sawing away on bended knee
Carpenters of the night.
They build their songs
Little ditties of holy
Out of thin air, some cartilage
And the truth.
See how the evening gown of heaven
Sequined with stars waltzes itself
Across the ballroom of sky
How the moon cups its ear
Rises to hear them.
The whole meadow turns out
Fireflies wink like lighters
Coyotes practice their scales
An acapella of frogs joining in from the pond.
And so the question becomes
At what point do you not stand up
And applaud? At what point
Do you not fall to your knees
And weep? Saying, "thank you, thank you"
To that eternally shy, famously invisible composer
Standing before of us all
Waving her silent baton.

Days Like These

The days are stacked against us
What good can we do?
Take note of everything
Be kind to animals
Bear down hard—that's my list.
Which is to say, we must earn our deaths
No half measures. This afternoon
Winter a ghost through the trees
Silence a white blanket of snow
Settling over the fields
There's nothing to lose, I'm going all in.
Just look at me, sitting here drinking my wine
The bright fall of light, the slow fall of snow
Making me incredibly happy.

Blessed Be

The closest I've come
to touching God
is holding a Rufous hummingbird
its tiny heart pounding
in the palm of my hand.

Aspen Grove

She chose to love all the world. The yellow aspen leaves rattling the air, sunlight leoparding the ground. There were the altruistic flowers, and the wind a longtime coming. All afternoon she'd sit with the purling stream a tickle in her ear, the blue sky so far, far away. In ones and twos she'd watch the aspen leaves release, twist, and sashay to the ground, watch the shadows stepping like cats from beneath the stones. At her feet coyote scat, and by the water the hoofprints of deer like tiny heartbeats pressed into the mud. Yes, night would come, winter would come, but she stayed, dreaming the world into the one she wanted. Call her any name you want: Sister, daughter, mother, grandmother; savior, friend, champion, hero.

The Desert is Full

Her idea was to walk sideways from life. All that there is. A light shirt, a pair of jeans, as much water as she could carry. She would set out for the horizon, "Isn't that what horizons are for?" Quietly she closed the door.

She walked for seven days into silence and space (the desert a poet's cottage), grew to know its winds and washes, its tightlipped lizards and rusted tin cans, the luck of the draw. Small birds came and went, shadows grew and retreated, she learned to mimic the breathing of snakes. Maybe it was all those bones bleached by the sun, maybe it was the umbrella of sky that sheltered, with each passing hour the vine of her worry withered, the plinth of her sadness crumbled.

As she walked, her name slowly came back, memories blossomed. "Outside the desert," she told an ancient mesquite on a hill, "there's a lifetime of noise." "Inside the desert," the mesquite told her, "there's so much space it becomes claustrophobic."

When she arrived home, she waited a week to wash the sand from her hair. She burned her journals in a ritual fire. Everyone could see she'd changed. She made friends more easily now, children and dogs came to greet her, birds would alight on her shoulder. Everything about her was light, light and loose, like something you might win at a fair. I saw her once, did I tell you? She smiled, took my hand with real care. She looked me straight in the eye. "The mesquite never moved," she said, "It just pointed the way."

Question

What
if it's not we
who forget
the names of the flowers
what if it's they
who forget us?

In the Closet of Great Happiness

In the closet of great happiness
I keep a small box of grief and regret
Simple reminder, note to self of the world as is.
Carved with a dull pocket knife
Chipped and nicked on the edges
Painted sky and blood-vessel blue
It owls-out the dark in hunger and silence.

I keep it on the very top shelf
Like the very best of liquors
But pushed to the back
Where it is hard to get to
And I must use a stool.
Come a winter's evening
Pewter light on silver snow
The wind a repeating verse of Never Look Back
I like to take it down and sit awhile
Think about the hallways of Mercy and Grace
What has been, could be
Never and always will.

I like the weight of it in my lap
The hand-smoothed sides
The cheap hinges, rusted now
Their small squeak of resistance.
Lined with green felt
Like fields to run through
The odor of cedar and Always Miss You remain
As does the welt of Hurt Beyond Repair.
All the while questions unanswered
There is no rhyme or reason. With eyes closed
I finger the contents one by one
Taste them with my tongue.

Make of this what you will
Make of it anything but untrue.
I am not a bitter man
Nor in the habit of melancholy
I only know happiness is a greased pig
Sadness and blame, low hanging fruit
And that everyone has this box
Large or small, new, or very old.
Which is why I rise and walk into the dark
Cross the cold clad fields
The icebound roads, stand a moment
On the riverbank of Never Forgetting
Offer my box to heaven
And the night bright stars.
Take this I say, take it and eat of me
For I am the sum of all my parts
And love is melting in the mountains.
True it may not be here soon, but will be again
And the river is wide.

A Dog's Head

To pat
a dog's head
run hand
over short
soft fur
trace ridge
of eyebrow
back between ears
feel the hard skull
gently cleaved
to palm this
perfection
troubles fade.

for Matt Taylor

Yellow Pine Chipmunk

When the warm heart of day
and thin wrist of luck
offer you a Yellow Pine Chipmunk
squatting on its haunches
cinnamon sides panting
in the phosphorus sun—take it.
Take it and its question mark tail
into your heart
its five black and white stripes
and forepaws clutched to its chest.
Take it and count your blessings
humble yourself before this tiny king
resting on its midden of cones
its polite wedge of face
a worn arrowhead
narrowing to twitching nose
and nonexistent chin.
For there is a world out there
larger than any imagined
with tiny paws
and a stop and go mentality.
Take it like you would take
your very last breath
and fill your cheeks
with the seeds of thanks
and mushrooms of praise
for that moment
when a pair of small
oil-drop eyes
look back into yours.

Grouse, Goshawk, Pine

The sharp-tailed grouse
dead in the talons of the goshawk
droops over the gray, twisted arm
of the wind-stunted pine.

The goshawk stands in profile
as if posing for a portrait, or coin
chest feathers gilded silver, black eye
the color of everything to come.

Victory can be spelled so many ways.
hunger is at the root of all things.
The goshawk turns his head this way and that.
Whatever made the grouse fly, has fled.

When I was young
I used to cry for the grouse, later
I learned to cheer the goshawk.
Now, I see little difference between the two.

Round and round we go, the sun
rising in the east, setting in the west.
The goshawk begins its meal.
The pine tree is old, wise, and strong.

Magpies

There are as many ways
To love the world
As there are ways
Of the world.
Today I'm watching magpies
Flying yin-yang clowns
Of the compost pile
Surfers of the backs of the cattle.
I watch them dining on road-kill
Stealing the cat food
Ordering the dog to stand down.
See how they come as if dressed for a party
Stalking the grounds in their feathered tuxedos.
You can almost see their minds spinning
Pissed off there isn't more food.
Really, what other species uses such language
Around their young?
But I won't let their conman ways fool me
As the light fades and the day goes
Wherever it is the day goes
I watch the magpies fly home
Long tail feathers brooming the wind
That tasteful splash of debonair blue on their backs
A grace note I will keep until morning.

In Search of What Matters

Here I am again, a bump on a log
Watching a beetle north by northwest
Trace the edge of a pond. Here I am
Taking my time with Time
In search of what matters
To birds, bees, this beetle
And the glass eye of the pond.
Ah, the present moment
Just an excuse to notice everything
The swallow's happy curve
The water's happy curve, the sky
Ridiculous with clouds.

When the Angels

When the angels come tripping out of the sky
All gossamer-winged, hiccupping light
Dressed in their finest Aurora Borealis
Shoes missing, halos askew, asking
"What is it like?" do you tell them

Time is a thief, Beauty a beggar
That heartache is the sound of your lover
Slipping out of bed. Do you tell them
The Devil walks Main Street
Dresses like you and me
And tells the funnier jokes, or that happiness
Is something they'll never get used to.

Do you mention Mercy doesn't sell well?
And how do you explain to beings
Who have never had ribs
Love hurts.

Oh, poor angels, look what it's come to
Nipple rings! Face tattoos!
Best then, not to go into detail
About the heart, or that fear
Is the local currency to use.
No, better to play dumb
(adjusting their shoulder straps out of decency as you do)
So that when they strike their harps
Thump their clouds
Chime in with voices like bells
About Love, you can beg their pardon
Stepping back, motioning to their ankles
Praying an explanation of gravity will do.

Perfectly

See how the ducks fit the marshes
How the hawks fit the sky
How the fish fit their rivers
And the bellies of bears.

See how the trees
Fit their forests, rocks fit the ground
How the deer fit their antlers
And their antlers the air.

Everything fitting everything
Exactly, completely, perfectly
The way stars fit the heavens
Sun fits the day, the way caves

Fit their mountains
And darkness fits its caves.
Have we learned nothing?
Think what it must be like

You, your whole life fitting itself—perfectly
The way wind fits the fields, fields
Fit the rain, the way rain fits the rivers
And open faces of flowers

The same way flowers fit your eye
And your eye fits the world
As does the world fit your heart
And your heart fits the world.

I Am the Eight-Year-Old Boy

To the woman in the buffet line
At the International Conference
For the Humane Treatment of all Living Things
When she asked me who I was, I said

I am the eight-year-old boy
who took the glass jar
from the kitchen counter
and postcard
from dining room table
and trapped the black and yellow
paper wasp
circling against the windowpane
and carried it outside
into the green freedom
of summer fields.

The First Word

How do the mountains not tumble
rivers back up
birds not fall from the sky
stunned with mourning?

Shouldn't the wolves be howling?
The clocks run backwards?
Why is the sky still blue?
This conspiracy of normal confuses me
I wander room to room.

I'm told "Mother"
is the first and last word
in every language.
Today it's the only word I know.

I look to the north, south, east, west
I look to the heavens and day-blind moon
I get down on my hands and knees.
My heart, I think I hear them
first the flowers, then the stars
shouting *Sally, Sally, Sally.*

Welcome, welcome, welcome home.

for Sally Stevens Finn, rest in peace

Poems Are Little Places

Poems are little places, tiny spaces
Where eternity lives. They are monks
Come down from the mountains
Into the cities. Poems don't tell us
The big things in our lives
Only the small, which are really the same.
They are doors
To Japanese teahouses
Just big enough for a warrior
Without armor to crawl through.
Reading a poem, get down on your knees
Crawl on your hands and knees
Knock on this door unknowing.
The door swings open
It rides on silent hinges, and who knows
What light comes from within.

We Are All God's Poems

We are all God's poems
The homeless man asleep in the doorway
Almost pastoral, the drunk on the subway
Free as free verse, the woman from Mexico City
Who laughs with her sister
In perfect rhyme. There's the tanka
Of gay couples, the senryu of Native boys
There's the junkie with a pretty smile
The prostitute with a pretty smile
The refugee from Syria with a pretty smile
All of them a narrative worth repeating
Like the newborn with Down Syndrome
(A beautiful haiku) and the girl at the checkout with braces
A couplet with the bagboy with acne
His mother a sonnet in the senior living facility
Trying to recall his name. Turn the page
We are all God's poems—lyric, epic—you a ballad
Me a limerick, dog-eared, coffee-stained
Every last one of us a love poem, just look, look!
At the anthology we make.

What Made You Stop

What made you stop
And turn to this page?
Was it the hope that beauty
Might succumb to a few careful words?
That my poem might support you
Through one more of God's days?
Or are you just one of those
Who can't live without words
The irresistible way
Black ink graces the page. I only ask
Because of a feeling I have
About what keeps you reading
Through these cable news days
When there's no work for poets
And their courtship of words
Their marriageable syllables
That keep you up through the night.
It's about love, isn't it.
The way flowers cough up
Their pink lungs of beauty
How the sun rips at them
With its insensible light
About the black boulder of bear
And flat even wind
About your own wild blooming
Silent voice from within
Everything important collapsing into words
Books bound together
Creation revealed, 26 letters
The ballpoint pen, humanness
On the black and white of each page
What the poets call life
And living symbols of truth
And whispers of stars
Tossed down in the night.

The Greatest Poem Ever Written

Three words
Scratched in the sand with a stick
With the tide coming in.

for Deborah

A Flawed Mortal Stumbling Toward Enlightenment

A flawed mortal stumbling toward enlightenment she walked under the barrel rolls of ravens. Eyes like sky, hair like sunset, she placed her faith in the ceremony of green, in blonde prairie grasses, in the consistently good decisions of mountains. She placed her trust where it belonged, on the ground, with the drift and haul of time-rubbed stones, the meandering paths of rivers and deer, the creaky wisdom of trees. "What good are we," she asked, "if we don't pray hard to everything?" That morning by the river, grasshoppers castanetting their wings, mergansers boating the weeds, a lone eagle turned on a gyre, passing its shadow over the water. To live in this world requires restraint, the saints say, mind like a river and the generosity of bees. She sat for a very long time, sun on her cheeks, sun on the pines, her happiness swinging on oiled hinges.

At the Bear Paw Battlefield

October 5th, 1877, after a 1,100–mile journey being chased by the U.S. Cavalry and only forty miles short of the Canadian border, the Nez Perce chief, Chief Joseph, laid down his arms. There, following a final five-day battle and siege he gave his immortal speech ending, "From where the sun now stands, I will fight no more forever."

The grasses lean this way and that
Sage knuckles the air
Winter slips between the coulees
Settles in for the year.

There's a tender song
Rising from the creek
And an old truth
Buried in the hills to the south.
A great man once stood here
Pointed to the sun and said
I will fight no more forever

Ah, these peaceful killing fields
A penny here, a penny there
A beer can left as offering
A toy horse as prayer
And then the wind, always
The wind
Repeating a song
Only the dead can hear.

The Abundance

Here the river
Never a wrong turn.

There the mountain
Holding up the sky.

I'm out for a walk
Sunlight on a crumple of water

The morning thick
with birdsong and leaves.

Nothing is out of place
Everything as it should be

Robins advertising spring
Mergansers like corks

There's the purl of water
And the work songs of bees.

A friend says, "Don't die before you die.
Live and live some more!"

I pull up a log, practice the art.
I watch a spider spinning its web

Watch the water striders
Perform their miracle.

To the Eight Dead Porcupines

You had the blackest eyes
And tiniest noses, your small paws

With their scimitar-like claws
Lying quietly open.

I found you this way, arranged
In a neat straight line, as if feigning sleep

But it was death you spooned
While the trash blew around you.

What did you ever do
To deserve this fate? What did you ever do

But cherish your young?
It was Saturday, sunlight and silence

In every direction, the prairie sky
Blind with distance. I knelt

To speak my gray words
And do what we do now

Which is nothing, take a picture
Call a friend, pluck a single, small quill

In honor, the eight of you
Mute as the day-flown moon, the north wind

Lifting your long, slender guard hairs
In perfect halos above you.

My Heart

I remember being taught in school
That the human heart is the size of a fist
A blood-filled muscle pounding
On the walls of the chest.
Oh, I was young
And had little experience in the world.
How could I know the terrors to come?
Crushing defeat, the hundred varieties
Of loss, the elephant of grief
Standing square upon the chest.
Still I think I did right
To raise my hand, clear my throat
And tell the wizened science teacher—"No"
The heart is the size of a prize-winning pumpkin
Yankee stadium, my father's Pontiac sedan.
The heart is an oak, straight and true.
The old man simply nodded
Smiled his more knowing smile
And let me walk home, happy as any boy could be
Proclaiming to the band of scholars that followed
My heart is Yosemite, the Himalayas
It is a blue whale surfacing
Plying the currents of life with joy
My heart is for all to see, the Taj Mahal
The Eiffel Tower, the Empire State Building.
My heart, I said, fists to my chest, is King Kong.

At the Dinner Party

The chatter of knives and forks
The need for napkins made known
Wine glasses fingerprinted and ruby kissed
The volume of laughter grows and grows.

The Wine Glass

The wine glass is empty
Now it is full.
I move a single strand of hair
Behind your ear.
The wine glass is empty
Now it is full again.

Cleaning the Dishes

Cleaning the dishes
after the dinner party
washing the wine glasses
placing them on the thin, white
cotton towel
for my wife to dry
she asks me
if I love her
and I tell her
about the silver snakeskin
I'd seen that morning
how beautiful it was
delicate and fine
as the shed wedding dress
I found twenty years ago
at the foot of the bed.

Old Money

The mountains ask for nothing
Flowers bloom for no coin
The poet is at his kitchen window
Rich beyond his wildest dreams
Chickadees at the feeder
Deer bedding down on the lawn.

for Robert Wrigley

Repeat After Me

Waking from a nap
I take great comfort in the knowledge
That everything is incomprehensible.

The river (obviously), the birch tree in the yard
(without a doubt), the two dark-eyed juncos
Canoodling in its branches.

Wiser men than me have said
Terrifying beauty surrounds us
And that the proper response

Is to weep with joy, have said
What we mustn't forget
Is we are made of old stars

And that our highest calling
Is to love with a ferocity
That knows no bounds.

Does this sound like something
You can do? Does it sound naive?
Then let it sound naive.

If there's only ever one prayer
You say for the rest of your life
Let it be thank you, thank you, thank you

Repeated over and over again.

All Night the Stars

All night
the stars
float down
the black river
it is an old story

I go out
into the night
into the black
to where the deer
come to drink them.

Such shy
graceful ladies
wading into
the heavens
such black noses

parting the night. I am speaking
of miracles
pale light
on their cheeks
pink tongues

licking the stars.
Is this not
what it's about?
Look, just there
moonlight cupping their ankles.

I Don't Know

I don't know
what prayer is

but I have seen dawn
and the long necks of deer

edging the meadow
I have seen hoofprints

like tiny soft heartbeats
pressed in the snow

and I have seen a spotted white fawn
drink from a river

and thought
maybe I do.

Do They Envy Us

Do they envy us? The angels?
Our cars that won't start
And angst over taxes?

Do they grow bored in heaven?
All that harp music
And endless cups of ambrosia.

Do they spend their days
Slamming fingers in doors
Or smashing their thumbs with hammers?

Anything, anything at all
To feel. And at night
When they take off their halos

Burying their faces
In the too soft clouds
Do they kneel before God

All sweetness and light
Begging—begging!—for one more chance
At a broken heart?

The Praises

I cannot sing enough the praises
Of the outer world and its gardens
But I have heard from the saints
And those who toil
In the grounds of the soul
About another garden, more spacious
And requiring no light.
They say it is a long way in
And a long way in
Is a circle. I believe them
And although I am not a gardener
And I am tired of walking in circles
I would like to make the journey
They say, I am a seed.

A Short List of Things to Wish For

Milkweed for Monarchs
Pollen laden bees
Glaciers to remain glaciers
That the trees understand.

Wish for snow in the mountains
Full rivers and streams
Wish cool temperatures for the trout
Wish for the trout.

Wish that our wishes amount to something
That our prayer be heard
Wish for the elephants, the oceans, death of the American lawn
Wish that the Constitution wasn't written in vain.

Wish for the bundle of rags on the park bench
That they wake to a warm place to stay
Wish for them courage in the face of all things
Wish them their dignity, and a new pair of socks.

Wish for the stars themselves, we need them more than they know
Wish for the shooting ones, wish they be many
Wish for the smallest among us, the little ones, the frail
Wish for the strength to defend them.

Wish that kindness becomes the new drug
Goodwill contagious
That you're as good as your dog thinks you are
For more time with your mother, your father.

Wish that love wasn't so hard
Wish for what pain teaches us, hard as that may be.
Wish for chance meetings with strangers
That they become friends.

Wish for forgiveness for the harm that you've done
Wish forgiveness of others, the harm they did you
Wish for silence and the ability to slow down
For long walks in the country with the sun going down.

Wish for more laughter
More laughter
More laughter
For an abundance of joy.

Wish for the innocence of children
The wisdom of elders
Wish that wherever you go
You are always at home.

Wish for the child hiding under their desk
Wish that the gun jams
Wish that this country comes to its senses
Wish God does the same.

Wish for health, happiness, and a swift painless death
Wish it for every creature and thing on this earth
Then wish for the day you don't have to make these wishes
Or anything even remotely like them ever again.

Building a Coffin

We know absolutely nothing
About death. We know precious little
About life. I spent today
Building a coffin, not a morbid day
Not a fancy coffin.

Another nail in the coffin, I'd say
And drive another one
Home. The saw ripping
Through the plywood, sweat
Dripping on the saw
I felt more alive than I had in years.

There can be pain mixed with joy
Mixed with sadness and grief.
There can be beliefs, right or wrong
That help us get through.
Looking out the window
On a handmade coffin in the sun
I think I did right to prop the lid open
And spread a layer of gold leaves on the bottom.

Because in winter we expect death
To be cold like our bones
In summer we picture death
As hell's hot burning fire.
I say a coffin should be a bright
And warm sunny place.

for Margaret and Malcolm Parker, rest in peace

Reincarnation

Lately I've been thinking
If I get my head straight
Play my cards right
Catch just the right god
On just the right day
Maybe I can come back as a lion.

Wouldn't that be something?
Paws thumping across the savanna
Napping in the African sun
Gold eyes, blonde mane, face
Bloodred chin-deep in a zebra.

Or maybe I can come back as a songbird
That seems easy enough
A song here, a song there
Then head south for the winter.

Or maybe the powers that be
Will let me back as a turtle
The ones butterflies flock to
Deep in the Amazon rainforest
Who perch on the heads of turtles
And drink the salt of their tears.

Oh, there's a hundred things I'd like to be
A hundred ways to skip out on heaven.
So let me come back as a cloud
Shouting thunder, throwing lightning
Scratching my belly on the tops of the trees.
I'll be a hat for the mountains
And a hose for the fields
Pouring everything I am
Back into the ground.

But wait, wait! I've got a better idea
Let me come back as a brook, say
One in New England, one a boy likes to walk to
A boy who sits on the banks in the late afternoons
Tosses rocks in and wades to the middle.
Let me take him by the ankles, the knees, the waist
Let him spread his arms and lean back into me
Let me be the one to float and support him
Let me be the one to wash away his troubles, his fears.

To Be a River

Ah to be a river
Fast running and smooth
Turbulent, calm, meandering
Friend to otter, beaver, and bear
To float the ducks, support the fish
Smooth the stones, to start small
And grow to something big.
I imagine spending the days
Passing the time by passing the trees
Running in rapids, resting in lakes
Curled in the eddies.
What a joy it must be
To flow alone, then join with others
To be the one, and be the many.
Yes, it is my dream to fall down mountains
Wander the valleys as I carve my own way
Never to look back, all the while
Giving all of myself to all that I am
And when the journey is over
To be that brave, empty myself
Without fear or foreboding
Into the very depths
Of my beginning.

This Wind

I would like to know about the wind
Not just any wind, *this wind*
The one here now, just arriving, just leaving
Not strong, not soft, a steady press
Against my chest, my face.

Where did it begin? *this wind*
Which is singular, and not.
I want to know what other travelers it has touched
What other trees, dogs, sides of barns
What birds it has lifted, and lakes rippled.

See how the leaves clap their approval
How the grasses curtsy and bow, *this wind*
Mountains smooth in its wake
With all the sky to run through
It takes the time to rustle my hair.

Oh, how I want to follow it
Over the forests, the fields
Find where it finally sets down
So that I might lie down with it, *this wind*
The two of us finally at rest, finally
At peace.

This Yellow Blanket

The genius of the morning
after so dark a night
slowly, so very slowly
first light slipping down the mountains
notching the tops of the trees
lighting the pastures, the fields.
Oh to be clad in this yellow blanket
birds singing.

In the Morning

...and then we will rise
and walk out into the garden
dressed only in sunlight
and the songs of birds, stand
before all creation, large and small
true to the love that made us
and I will take your hand
and you will take my hand
and we will smile the very first smiles
laugh the very first laughs
we did as children
fresh from that other garden
our mothers' wombs
and all the years since
and all the years to come
will be as one
and have no power over us
for we will have each other
and in our having
we will have all.

My Last Wish

When my time comes
Whatever you do, please
Don't waste a good hole, instead
Prop me up in the meadow
Lean me against that old maple tree
Sing songs, get drunk, laugh, dance
I don't care, just make sure Coyote can find me
To bring a leg bone back to the den.
Better yet, place me in a pine box
Made of old boards nobody wants
Roast me on a fire down by the river
Let me be smoke and sparks
That rise in the night, and in the morning
Push what's left into the water
So I can say goodbye to the fishes.
But really, really, my dying wish
Is haul me to a mountaintop
Face me east, leave me there
Because it will be the hardest thing
I ever do, to leave this place
And I'll want to see the sunrise
One last time.

Miracles Happen

There is a wonderful truth out there
I can see it swaying in the branches.
There is an ocean of good, I believe
Melting in the mountains. There is hope
Inside every seed, and greatness sown
In every breath of air.
Can you see it? I can see it.
Please, the world is counting on us.
We must all believe. Take my hand, I will take yours
Let us make love, let us walk on the water.

A Note on the Places That Inspired Some of These Poems

As any reader can see, I have a deep connection to Montana and the Northwest as a whole—it is home in every sense of the word—and I'm often asked about the places that inspired my poems. Most are set in Montana, some in Oregon, and a few elsewhere that bring me the same feeling of home.

This addition is my attempt to provide readers signposts to the places that inspired a number of the poems. Whether I was physically in that place at the time of writing, or later travelling through it in my mind's eye, I hope these notes bring you closer to the landscape, and the poems, as they did me.

Driving the Backroads of Montana

"Driving the Backroads of Montana" is not about a particular place or specific backroad, rather it's a combination of all the backroads I've driven in Montana. Still, even though I say that, if I had to pin it down, I'd say I was thinking of the gravel dirt roads just north of Havre; those long, straight, flat, seemingly endless dirt roads that parallel Highway 2, or even the ones further north, along the Canadian border. I love driving these roads—windows down, sun and warm air coming in. You can go for miles without passing another vehicle. All there is is a line of telephone poles and a barbed wire fence running beside you, maybe a farmhouse here or there and then way off in the distance another, and between them nothing but fields and fields of wheat and wind and not a lot more.

Coyote / And So It Is / Simple Pleasures / A Flawed Mortal Stumbling Towards Enlightenment

Like birds, rivers play a large part in this book, the Blackfoot and the Deschutes in particular, but none more so than the Milk River. The Milk River, for those who don't know, leaves from Glacier National Park and takes a turn up into Canada, then comes back down into Montana and wanders through Havre before eventually entering the Missouri below Fort Peck. It's a murky, slow moving, shallow river, perfect for sitting on its banks and pondering life. Driving out River Road on the northside of Havre and parking at what's called the Rookery is probably the place I go on the most regular basis.

I walk along the Milk River at least once a week, if not more, and poems like "Coyote" are taken directly from its banks. In this case, a few winters ago, I saw one of the most beautiful coyotes I'd ever seen, his winter coat, which was very blonde, full and gleaming, catching the low winter light. He was crossing the ice not too far downstream from where I stood and stopped to look at me.

And then there are the more general poems about the Milk, such as "And So It is", "Simple Pleasures", and "A Flawed Mortal Stumbling Toward Enlightenment." I wrote all three of these sitting on my front porch, thinking about the Milk and the walks I'd take there. All of these grew out of my time at the river, taking it all in, taking in the morning and all that was around me.

Prairie Wind / This Wind

I've lived most of my life in the mountains, or at least very near mountains, where I had easy access to them. So moving to Havre and living on the prairie was quite different. People often say that the prairie is boring, flat, and lacking in beauty. But in the short time I've lived here, I've fallen in love with the place—the light and the different colors of the fields, of course the big sky, but also the Bears Paw Mountains and the scattered badlands.

Another thing that people say about Havre is that it's windy. I've never lived in a place that is anywhere near as windy as it is here. So naturally, I had to write a couple poems about the wind. "Prairie Wind" and "This Wind" are my homage to what can sometimes feel like the near constant winds you encounter. As I was writing both of these, I was thinking of where the winds originate, the Front Range of the Rockies or vague points north in Canada, then imagining how it travels over towns like Browning and Cut Bank and Shelby, making its way east before eventually reaching Havre and my front porch. And then I'd picture everything to the east, how the wind would keep going, to

Chinook (named for a wind now that I think of it) and on to Malta and Wolf Point and eventually the Dakotas. I suppose I imagine the wind, not just in one place as I experience it, but everywhere.

Listen Closely

Probably my favorite place in Montana, in fact my favorite place in the world, is my cabin in Potomac. I built it close to 20 years ago, a perfect little writing retreat set off in a stand of ponderosas at the end of Blixit Creek Road. The cabin is off-grid, no electricity or running water, just a wood stove for heat and a small two-burner propane stove to cook on. The entire place is made with reclaimed lumber and materials. It's small by any standards, 8' by 12' with a sleeping loft above a small porch. No matter the season, it's always such a joy to spend time there. "Listen Closely" was written on a summer evening when I'd crawled up to the loft and opened the window. I was enjoying the night air and the sounds of the forest; that little bit of wind in the trees, the kind of thing that makes you feel like you can hear near anything if you listen hard enough, and that's what kicked off the poem.

Geese, North in the Spring

As with my previous book, *On a Benediction of Wind,* there are a number of bird poems in this volume, either directly about birds or referencing them one way or another. So it should come as no surprise to anyone who knows Montana, and especially if they've heard of Freezeout Lake just outside of Choteau, to find out that, "Geese, North in the Spring" was written about the geese there. I try to get there every year, either in the fall or the spring, or both if I'm lucky, to watch the incredible migration of snow geese, tundra swans, trumpeter swans, you name it; literally tens of thousands of birds. My wife and I will go down and we'll spend the night and get up before dawn and watch what they call "the great liftoff", thousands of birds taking off at the same time to head north or south on the next leg of their journey. Visually it's stunning, but it's the sound too, the very definition of cacophony. "Geese, North in the Spring" isn't really about one particular time I was there, it's the combination of all the times I've been and watched this amazing migration. If you ever get the chance, if you're ever in Montana for those few weeks when the birds are passing through, make sure you go see it.

Yellow Pine Chipmunk

There's a walking trail outside of Bend, Oregon called Benham Falls. It's a great place to go, especially when it's really hot because there's a shaded path that runs alongside the river. I was walking there one day when I came to a small promontory overlooking the whitewater below. To my surprise, I saw a chipmunk sitting there too, with his back to me, looking out over the water in a private reverie of sorts. I know I'm anthropomorphizing, but it looked as if he was just taking it easy, kicking back, enjoying the beauty of the day and the cool mist that was coming up off the water, much like I was.

Perfectly

Shortly after we were married, my wife and I moved to Stevensville, Montana. We lived there for a couple of years and rented a place right on the edge of the Lee Metcalf National Wildlife Refuge, and because we lived so close I got to spend a lot of time there. I might go for an hour or two. Sometimes all day if I could. I would hang out and watch the ducks and the osprey, the deer, porcupines, muskrats, whatever, just hang out with my notebook. There's a series of ponds there with all kinds of bird life, and the Bitterroot River makes up the western boundary of the refuge. On the opposite side of the river is the massive wall of the Bitterroot Mountains. The whole place is beautiful. It's what inspired the poem "Perfectly." Just sitting there writing down what I saw and what I was thinking, how nature was uncomplicated and everything seemed to work so well together— perfectly, in fact.

The Abundance

If you're driving from Potomac to Missoula on Highway 200, there's a number of fishing access sites along the Blackfoot River, places you can pull over and get down to the water. My favorite is the Angevine access. Whenever I'm heading into Missoula from my cabin, I try to schedule a little extra time to stop there. I'll take a book or my notebook and just sit on the bank, watching the water slide by. If it's warm enough, I might go for a swim. It's something I like to do before entering what I'll call the "fray" of Missoula. "The Abundance" reminds me of all the times I'd stop and sit there, watching the sunlight lighting up the larch trees on the far bank, and of course, admiring the water striders oaring in the eddies.

Author's Note:

There's a widely held belief that artists—poets in particular—are solitaries, slaving away in isolation, holed-up in their little writing shack or room, turning out works of beauty and grace from the depths of their tortured and lonely souls.

Nothing could be further from the truth.

I would like to thank my family, especially my three siblings, Deborah, Alan, and Janet, whose love and support over what has literally been a lifetime has kept me going. Who could have predicted "the kid" of the family would amount to anything, much less a poet.

A deep and heartfelt thank you to our late parents and late sister, Mary. If you see good in me, it is because of them.

I'd like to thank my friends—saints and sinners all—who encouraged me, showed me kindness, and bought me beer these many years. To everyone in the communities of Havre and Missoula, Montana; Bend, Oregon; Kaslo and Argenta, British Columbia, no one is more blessed than I am to have such quality people in their life.

To the community of Waterbury, Vermont, in the 1960's, 70's and early 80's. There was no better place to grow up. To Syracuse University and the friends I made there, thank you. To David Paul at David English House in Hiroshima, Japan, and all who worked there and passed through, *arigato gozaimasu.*

To our cats, Rilke and Tija, you bring me joy on a daily—no, hourly—basis. I love you so. And to the ones who came before, Lutsa, Pushkin, Dash Point, and the one who started it all, 42. How much less my life would have been without you.

I would like to say thank you to the Milk River, The Blackfoot River, The Deschutes and the Winooski, as well as a very special thank you to Thatcher Brook in Waterbury, Vermont, and Kootenay Lake in Argenta, British Columbia. With you (and in you) I found peace and solace. To the Green Mountains, The White Mountain, The Cascades, Goat Range, and Purcells, to the lovely Bear Paws, walking your spines, rubbing my head on the sky, you made me the best I could be.

Thank you to every bird that sang to me or visited, to every deer, rabbit, racoon, butterfly, bee, and bear that graced me with their presence or sight. And to the trees I have known, not the least of which the maple in the backyard of my best friend's house, Mike Eastman, growing up, and the Ponderosa pines in Potomac, MT that to this day shelter my cabin.

Here's to all the More Than Human World—sun, moon, stars, wind, rain—to every breathing, growing, and living thing, thank you. You are inspiration and more than inspiration, you are life itself.

Thank you to my literary heroes: Rainer Maria Rilke, Mary Oliver, Annie Dillard, Peter Matthiessen, Barry Lopez, Henry Beston, and James Agee (to list just a few), I stand in your shadow and bow before you.

To the writing community of the Pacific Northwest, you welcomed me in and I have never experienced anything but your encouragement and support. This includes Elizabeth Quinn, who entrusted me with *High Desert Journal,* and to everyone it brought me in touch with, staff, contributors, and readers. I believe we did good.

Thank you, of course, to the editors of the fine journals listed in the back matter that published me along the way and published many of the poems that appear in this edition. Thank you for sharing my work with a wider audience, which is ultimately all a poet can ask or hope for.

A very sincere thank you to Phil, Annie, Molli, Anna, and the entire staff at Chatwin Books. Your attention to detail and commitment to beauty is second to none. Thank you for taking a chance on me. And to my good friend and wonderful pastel artist Bobbie McKibbin, for her wonderful cover art.

And to you, the readers, both known and unknown, thank you. For you and because of you, I strive to do my best.

Finally, I want to thank my wife. There is no stronger woman I know. You are steel and sunshine, you make everyone's life better just by being you, and you make everyone happier just by stepping into the room—but none so more than me. Twenty-one years and counting. This book, these poems, would truly not be if not for you. Thank you. I love you.

—Charles Finn, Havre, MT, spring 2025

Acknowledgements

Thank you to the editors of the following journals where these poems first appeared, sometimes in slightly different versions.

Driving the Backroads of Montana, Memory's Anvil, *Big Sky Journal*
Simple Pleasures, *Deep Wild Journal*
And So It Is, All Together Now, Aspen Grove, *Abandoned Mine*
Prairie Wind, *Bear Paw Arts Journal*
Song Sparrow, Sunday Morning, In the Café, Ever Since I Can Remember, *New England Writers Anthology*
Snail Mail, *Conservative Review*
Yellow Pine Chipmunk, *Cascadia Field Guide*
Poems Are Little Places, What Made You Stop, *Byline*
We Are All God's Poems, *We Are All God's Poems Anthology*
The Praises, *Afterthoughts*

photo: Barbara Michelman

CHARLES FINN is author of *Wild Delicate Seconds: 29 Wildlife Encounters*, and *On a Benediction of Wind: Poems and Photographs from the American West*, winner of the 2022 Montana Book Award. He is co-editor of the textbook/anthology *The Art of Revising Poetry: 21 U.S. Poets on Their Drafts, Craft, and Process*, as well as co-editor of the poetry anthology, *We Are All God's Poems.* He lives in Havre, MT, with his wife Joyce Mphande-Finn and their two cats, Tija and Rilke.